About This Book

Title: *Rocks*

Step: 1

Word Count: 65

Skills in Focus: All short vowels

Tricky Words: Earth, outside, some, you, find, are, parks

Ideas For Using This Book

Before Reading:
- **Comprehension:** Look at the title and cover image together. Ask readers what they know about rocks. What new things do they think they might learn in this book?
- **Accuracy:** Practice saying the tricky words listed on page 1.
- **Phonemic Awareness:** Look at the title and help students blend the sounds. Have readers listen as you segment the sounds in the word *rocks* (/r/, /o/, /ck/, /s/). Ask readers what the word is and what short vowel sound they hear in the word. Repeat with other words found in the text, having readers identify the short vowel sound in each word. Suggested words: *big, lots, sacks, tan, tub*.

During Reading:
- Have readers point under each word as they read it.
- **Decoding:** If readers are stuck on a word, help them say each sound and blend the sounds together smoothly. Be sure to point out any short vowel sounds.
- **Comprehension:** Invite students to talk about what new things they are learning about rocks while reading. What are they learning that they didn't know before?

After Reading:
Discuss the book. Some ideas for questions:
- What kinds of rocks have you seen before? What do they look like?
- What do you still wonder about rocks?

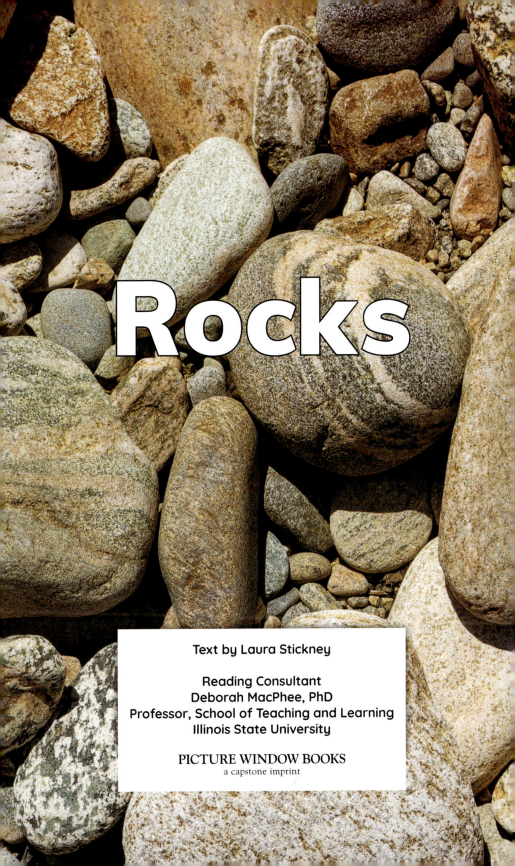

Rocks

Text by Laura Stickney

Reading Consultant
Deborah MacPhee, PhD
Professor, School of Teaching and Learning
Illinois State University

PICTURE WINDOW BOOKS
a capstone imprint

Earth has lots of rocks.

Rocks can be big.

But some rocks are not.

Kids can pick up rocks outside.

Kids can pan for rocks at parks.

Pick up rocks in sand.

Pick up rocks in mud.

Put rocks in bags.

Pack rocks in sacks.

You will find
lots of rocks.

Set rocks in tubs.
Get rocks wet.
Rub the muck off.

Rocks are fun!

More Ideas:

Phonemic Awareness Activity

Practicing Short Vowels:
Tell readers to listen as you stretch the sounds of a short vowel word. Starting at your shoulder, move your hand while tapping down your arm (i.e., shoulder-elbow-wrist) as you say each sound slowly. The students will call out the word. Repeat and have students say the sounds with you, moving their hand down their opposite arm as they say the sounds. Blend the sounds together smoothly to make the word. Have readers slide their hand smoothly down their arm as they blend the word. Have readers finger-trace the short vowel letter in the air.

Suggested words:
- rock
- mud
- lot
- wet
- kid

Extended Learning Activity

Rock Scavenger Hunt:
Have readers go outside and look for different rocks. After readers have collected their rocks, ask them to write a sentence about how each rock looks or feels. Challenge students to use words with short vowel sounds in their sentences.

Published by Picture Window Books, an imprint of Capstone
1710 Roe Crest Drive, North Mankato, Minnesota 56003
capstonepub.com

Copyright © 2026 by Capstone.
All rights reserved. No part of this publication may be reproduced in whole or in part, or stored in a retrieval system, or transmitted in any form or by any means, electronic, mechanical, photocopying, recording, or otherwise, without written permission of the publisher.

Library of Congress Cataloging-in-Publication Data is available on the Library of Congress website.

ISBN: 9798875226939 (hardback)
ISBN: 9798875229060 (paperback)
ISBN: 9798875229046 (eBook PDF)

Image Credits: iStock: aamorim, 22–23, AlukardS, 17, Blacqbook, 12–13, G Eddie Patten Sr, 20–21, kaz_c, 10, ktaylorg, 1, 18–19, Maestrovideo, 16, Meinzahn, 6, 24, simonkr, 14–15, Wirestock, cover; Shutterstock: Andrew Berezovsky, 2–3, Cynthia A Jackson, 11, Irisland, 7, Mark van Dam, 8–9, nadia_if, 4–5

Printed and bound in China. 6274